THE TRANSPORTED SOUL

A JOURNEY TO YOU

By Maria Certo

Designed and Illustrated
By Suzanne Pell

Introduction

For as long as I can remember, I have had this deep passion to share with others what lives inside of me.

One day, in the early nineties, I was taking a walk around Niagara Falls, when suddenly I heard in my right ear, "You are going to write a book."

I laughed and thought "that is silly."

I asked myself, "what would I write a book about?"

I knew it could not be about my retired profession as an Occupational Therapist.

I enjoyed and am grateful for my work as an OT, but knew it was not a deep passion of mine that would inspire me to author a book.

I also knew that what I received came from spirit but had no idea what the book would entail.

I let it go, but never forgotten the message spirit had given to me that day.

If you were guided to this book, my deepest desire is that it will inspire you to be who YOU truly are!

You will come to understand that your reality with the traumatizing experiences of abuse, whether it be sexual, verbal, emotional or physical, will give birth to your soul's requirements.

It will reveal to You what your heart knows to be true and that is that YOU do not deserve to be abused, ever!

YOU are a beautiful infinite soul who came here to live a healthy life of love, peace, truth and joy and to experience all that YOU are!

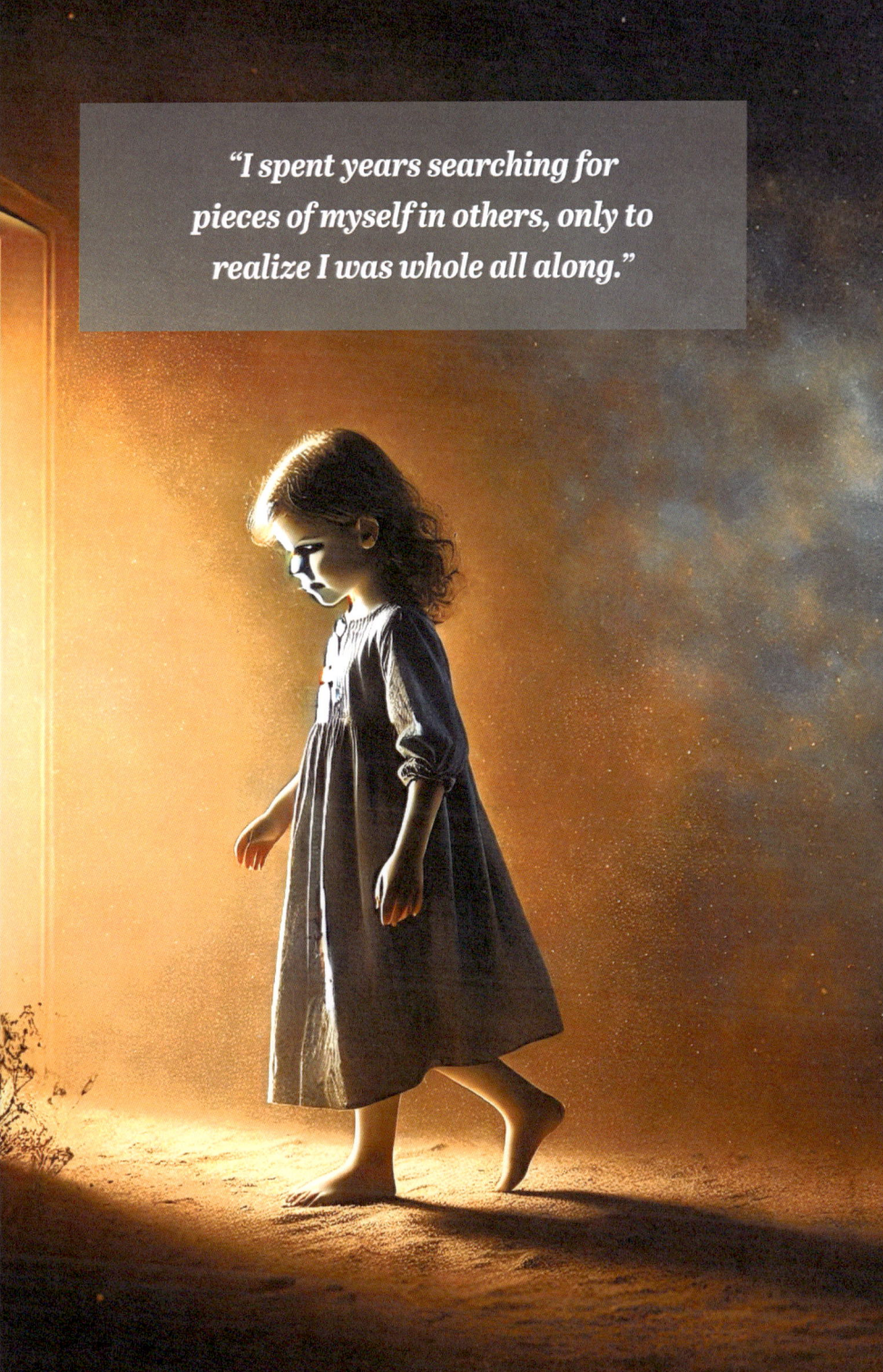

"I spent years searching for pieces of myself in others, only to realize I was whole all along."

"The past lingers in the quiet moments, whispering doubt, but I am learning to answer with strength."

Forward

I had a history riddled with sexual, emotional, verbal and physical abuse, beginning in childhood, and working its way through adulthood. The life I lived at was one of denial and victim mentality.

I grew up with those who held no responsibility for the negative choices that they made.

This was etched into my subconscious and resulted in learned behaviors.

I did not love nor cared for myself.

I was insecure and confused on which road to go down.

I had no compass guiding me in which turn to take to find who I truly was.

I felt lost.

In life I made poor decisions based on my relationships from the past.

A past plagued with abuse and a mind that was corrupted with confusion.

I learned that my choices in relationships mirrored those who abused me on a variety of levels. I had to play out these patterns to be able to see them.

I needed to take ownership of my choices and be responsible for my own hand in the empty life I had been living.

I had to take down the walls I had built around me and begin to allow love to flow through me.

The love I did not receive. I had to find it within me and give it to myself.

It took time before I was able to acknowledge my soul's light.

Every time an attack happened, whether it be sexual, emotional, verbal, or physical, I lost a part of me.

With each passing day, I felt a deep endless pit of sorrow, drama, and confusion.

Through every trial, I gained wisdom.

I became wise to others negative intentions, none which belonged to me.

I made the mistake of taking on their pain and making it mine.

In the end, I had no idea who I was and why my life was empty.

I finally went inward and dealt with the issues I had ignored for decades.

I had to uncover each layer until I reached the core of my being, my soul.

I made the decision to take care of me.

I chose to love myself.

"Pain taught me how to survive. But now, I am teaching myself how to live."

Chapter 1

The Early Years

When I was five, my father molested me.

I did not recall the sexual abuse until I was in my late thirties.

I began having flashbacks, memories and feelings that kept flooding into my awareness.

My earliest memory that poured through me was when I was lying in bed alone, at age 5 and seeing the ceiling come down towards me. I thought the ceiling was going to crush me.

I was terrified.

In retrospect, seeing the ceiling come down on me was a direct correlation to having my father force himself on me.

This became clear why I had the experience of the intense fear of the ceiling falling towards me and feeling as though I was going to be crushed.

I would also see those animated characters from the sixties, Gumby, and Pokey, sitting on my nightstand, looking straight at me. That was my favorite cartoon in childhood at that time.

Looking back, they came through to me for comfort during a time when I held great confusion and fear

"Every scar carries a story. Every story holds a lesson. And every lesson shapes the person I am."

as a little girl.

I still can see and feel the images in my minds eye of the ceiling falling towards me and Gumby and Pokey on my nightstand. Their impressions left an imprint into my consciousness.

I remember feeling that the images I had witnessed had a "sizzling "look to them. It was not solid, rather they had a liquified energy feel to them.

When this happened, I would run into my parents' room and wake my mother up to tell her how frightened I was.

My mother would tell me I was having a nightmare and to go back to sleep.

It truly was a living nightmare, unbeknown to my mother at that time I was bringing these scary incidents to her attention.

I also recalled hiding under the bed at five years of age, masturbating regularly to gain that pleasurable feeling I had known from my father who had me perform oral sex on him. He also fondled and performed oral sex on me.

"Some wounds don't show on the surface, but they shape us all the same. Healing begins the moment we stop running from our own truth."

I knew masturbating was a secret I had to keep.

Just as I knew I had to keep the secret of molestation, which I had been hiding for years.

Memories continued to resurface.

One memory that came to me was the time I told two neighborhood boys, who were playing outside in front of my house, to pull down their pants and touch themselves.

I was ONLY 5 when I asked them to do that!

Just writing this brings up feelings of shame, which I carried with me for years.

Thankfully, the neighborhood boys did not comply with my request.

Asking them to do such a vile act was rooted in what I learned at that time. That is what was normal for my experience. I did not know any better.

It truly is unimaginable that the purity of a 5-year-old could hold that image in their mind and attempt to play it out with another.

My father's sick choice to molest me damaged my psyche and affected my entire life for years to come.

Broken Trust

The trauma of sexual molestation becomes etched in your mind.

It becomes the imprint of unhealthy patterns to follow.

When you have experienced molestation by someone whom you trust, your psyche becomes garbled with misinformation on what love truly means.

Given these mixed signals early in childhood, confusion takes a hold of the mind and heart.

It will manifest itself in unusual ways, one in which it will rear its ugly face on a variety of levels. In my case it revealed itself in personal relationships and not taking care of my own needs in loving myself.

Over the years I found myself connecting to those whom I could not trust nor to those who did not truly care for my heart.

These patterns would play out for years.

"Healing isn't about erasing the past—it's about finding the courage to rewrite the future."

Chapter 2

Hidden Anger

As a little girl, I recall times where my father would try to kiss me hello or goodbye.

I would swipe my hand swiftly and roughly across my mouth in disgust.

Later in life when I looked back at those times when he kissed me, it became clear why I had such a strong reaction.

I was ANGRY!

The day of the molestation, my father took me for a ride in his car. What would happen next would change the trajectory of my life for many years to come.

It shattered my soul into a million different fragments.

My innocence was stolen at an early age.

I felt broken.

He had me perform oral sex on him while he did the same to me after fondling me.

On the night of the horrifying sexual abuse, we were driving back home, when I started to look out the window from the back seat of the car.

I saw small screens standing on tall singular poles, every few miles.

They resembled television screens which were along the side of the road.

Each small screen was playing a movie of sorts.

Repressed Emotions

In retrospect, I tried to go somewhere in my mind to

repress the terrifying experience of having to perform oral sex at the age of five on him and be a receiver of it.

Seeing those movie screens along the side of the road was a way to block the terror I had felt after the abuse.

Just as the images of the ceiling falling towards me when I was lying in bed and the animated characters, Gumby and Pokey sitting on my nightstand starring at me.

They were all images created out of fear, terror and trauma.

When we have experienced abuse of any kind, we repress our deepest painful emotions, they will reveal themselves in unexpected ways.

Anxiety, shame, confusion, guilt, depression, denial and anger will show up in our lives.

I have experienced all of them throughout my childhood and adult life.

Anxiety has been my closest friend.

It kept me awake at night with constant worries about those I love.

It created riffs in my relationships over the years because of my inability to let go and trust in myself and in the process of life.

This anxiety was related to the unhealed part of myself that was grounded in sexual abuse.

I did not feel safe nor protected as a little girl.

These feelings of being unprotected created anxiety. I led an unhealthy emotional life.

When we carry these repressed emotions our life choices become tainted.

Suffering continues not only with yourself, but it is also transferred to others.

"*Even in the darkness, there were always glimpses of light. I just had to remember how to see them.*"

"Letting go doesn't mean forgetting. It means choosing peace over pain, freedom over fear."

Chapter 3
Emotional Set Points

Emotional Set Points
Our emotions drive our decisions.

They direct us throughout the healing process. They are messengers letting us know we are out of balance and alignment with our true selves.

When we are out of balance our confusion creates unwise choices, missing God's message.

When there is unresolved anger, we lash out at others, regretting it later.

When we feel sad, we shut off those we love, missing what we need most, the receiving of that love.

When we feel anxious, overreaction is predictable and more pain results.

When you feel unworthy, seeing your value is impossible.

I have felt these emotions when I was off center throughout my life.

They taught me the importance of finding balance.

Aligning the Heart.

The road to balancing our emotions when you have suffered abuse, lies in the center of your heart.

This balancing act of the heart is analogous to walking a tight rope across Niagara Falls with the use of a stick to hold you upright.

If you turn the stick too far to the left or to the right, you will lose your balance and fall off into the rapids.

Chaos breaks out and you start drowning in your emotions waiting for the life preserver to float by to save your life.

If you remain calm and pay close attention to the importance of each step ahead, mindfulness will occur.

I aligned my emotions throughout the years with the lessons I learned along the way.

I was able to release the anger I held inside and found my center.

I acknowledged my value and found love for who I am.

"The hardest thing I ever did was stop waiting for an apology that would never come and start giving myself the closure I deserved."

"There was a time I thought healing meant going back to who I used to be. Now I know it's about becoming who I was meant to be."

Chapter 4
Putting the Pieces
of the Puzzle Together

Throughout the years, while gathering wisdom along the way through each lesson learned, I became aware of the choices I made in life that mirrored my upbringing.

I began to have insight into why I did the things I did that brought me to those decisions.

The human condition is a delicate one. One that teaches us how to behave and links our psyche to poor choices in establishing relationships with others when we have suffered abuse.

I began to understand, after I had freed myself from the blockages that I had placed in my mind and heart, that the choices I made in relationships of all kinds reflected my perception of love.

I realized that I had sought out relationships that echoed my past and subconsciously chose them.

I learned that if I were to live a life of healthy love, I had to cleanse these patterns of behavior that dragged me down into the mud.

These patterns of abuse taught me how to be a victim.
They instructed me in how to be controlling.
They showed me how to live a life of denial and how to ignore ownership of my own choices.
They directed me in how to be angry.
These patterns opened the doors for the cycle of abuse to continue in my life.

Learned Behaviors
I am a Psych-K® Facilitator.
It is a spiritual process with psychological benefits.
I work with clients to facilitate and dismantle limiting beliefs that are held subconsciously from learned behaviors in childhood and throughout one's life.

When you experience abuse, you can sense behaviors in relationships that bind you to those who replicate the same back to you. They enter your subconscious mind and create beliefs that play out in life.

What became clear was that I was unconscious about who I was. I found certain negative behaviors of my past in the relationships I had been part of over the years and surprisingly, I also found all of them inside of myself.

I learned denial.
I played this out for so long, until finally I discovered what I was hiding. I was hiding from myself.

"I no longer measure my worth by what I endured. I measure it by the strength it took to rise."

This taught me how to take ownership in my life with every choice I made.

I learned how to be a victim.

Choosing to be a victim in the abusive relationships that I held onto created a deep void inside.

I was a victim for years talking about my story of betrayal by others.

I am certain I exhausted all those who would listen to me.

I could not get out of my own way, no matter what others may have been trying to tell me, to help me, I was not ready to receive it.

I was so stuck being a victim, I forgot how to live a happy life.

I could not make sense of any of it.

I could not understand how someone you are supposed to trust could choose to make you feel dismissed and unloved.

I felt devalued on so many levels.

Making a conscious choice to not be a victim showed me how to stand on my own and to stop blaming the past or those in it for the miserable life I was living.

Remaining the victim is unbecoming and suppresses the elevation of your soul.

Staying in this unhealed state clouds your true self.

I learned control.

I tried to control things, this way I did not have to

"Not everyone will understand your journey, and that's okay. You are walking a path meant only for you."

"It's okay to be a work in progress. Every step forward is still a step toward something better."

face my hidden fears.

Being controlling helped me stay in the safe zone of denial.

What I learned was that attempting to control things kept me chained to false hope.

The lessons of control were plentiful. Surrendering control, showed me how to face my inner demons and fears.

Releasing control taught me how to let go of things that were never meant to be in the first place.

I learned anger, which in turn taught me how to live a life with resistance within me to forgive.

When I finally released the hidden anger, lessons of self-forgiveness and self-compassion appeared.

These were some of the greatest lessons on my journey.

I am grateful for each one.

They set my soul free.

Chapter 5

The Pain of Others

"When someone shows you who they are, believe them the first time".

-Maya Angelou-

The Pain of Others

In relationships of all kinds,when someone's pain is unhealed, you become their target.

This is how abuse begins.

They project their hurt and anger towards you, sometimes they are unaware of their transference.

The problem gets larger when the abused communicates their needs and remains unheard.

This is when the breakdown of the relationship crumbles and the person abused feels unloved and wants to exit the relationship.

The abused feels emotionally and sometimes physically unsafe.

I have felt this in relationships in life.

The abuse escalates because the abuser begins to lose control.

This cycle repeats itself until the relationship comes to an end.

"For so long, I searched for someone to save me. Then I realized—I was the hero I had been waiting for."

Each person needs to be responsible for the choices they are making for the health of their life.

Surfacing Emotions

The abused may react strongly with anger because for so long they had been silenced during the abuse and finally reach a breaking point and unleash their anger towards the abuser.

It isn't pretty. The abused person reacts negatively to the abuser and lashes out towards them. This happens because the abused person throughout the duration of the relationship was not being heard nor were the behaviors of the abuser changing.

The confusion and pain become overwhelming.

Holding in these unreleased emotions from long standing abuse causes the abused to forget how to honor and love themselves. They also forget how to remain centered and non-reactive.

You continue to reside in the web of misplaced emotions.

I participated in this loop of unreleased emotions throughout the years in relationships.

It inhibited the growth of my soul.

This had been my reality since I was a child.

My map to what true love was misdirected early in childhood. It brought me down a path of illusions, unhealthy love, betrayal and abuse.

In the process, I forgot about me. I forgot to love myself.

Chapter 6

Confrontation

I was 43 years old when I found the courage to confront my father.

I had recalled the sexual abuse and kept it to myself for a few years, after recalling it, waiting and wondering when it would be a suitable time to bring it out in the open.

I knew not only would it change my life, but it would also change the lives of those affected by the truth.

I received a phone call from my father.

I answered the phone, and he said, "Maria, your daughter got a traffic ticket, and she is irresponsible, just like her mother!"

This infuriated me and became the trigger point for me to speak the truth.

Teenagers need to learn through their mistakes, but to call her irresponsible and then to compare her to me, stating the same, was the end all for me!

I said, "Irresponsible"?! "You are the one who is irresponsible"!

He said, "What are you talking about"?

I answered, "The day you molested me, that was not only irresponsible, but evil"!

"The weight I carried was never mine to hold. I am finally setting it down."

In that moment he called out to my mother saying, "Maria said I molested her."

I asked him why he was involving her. I told him, "I am not talking to mom, I am talking to you"!

Then he asked me, "What did we do"?
I said, "You know what YOU did."

He persisted in asking what we did.

I felt like vomiting and said to him, "We had oral sex."

I was shocked by his question of "what did we do"?

I couldn't believe he asked that because it entailed the sexual abuse that both of us performed oral sex on each other, which serves the question, "what did WE do"?

He wanted to see if I recalled the sexual abuse correctly.

He said, "I wasn't attracted to you."

My mouth was hanging open. I could not believe what I heard.

I replied, "What are you saying, you weren't attracted to me, that is sick"!

He said, "If that is true, how come it didn't happen all the time."

His reactions were stunning!

I never told him the frequency of the molestation, only that it happened.

I said, "I never told you how often it happened."

The truth is that I only recalled one time, which affirmed his reaction and statement about "If that is true, why didn't it happen all the time"?

He then said, "Your mother was always home." I replied, "She wasn't around that day."

Then he said, "You waited 40 years to bring this up"? I replied, "Yes."

He thought he got away with his actions and never thought it would come out to the forefront.

He never denied it during the entire conversation, Instead, his reactions to the confrontation spoke loudly!

An extremely wise and trusted friend once told me, "The truth always catches up with the soul."

This was the moment of TRUTH!

After the confrontation with him, my mother got on the phone.

I was close to her and loved her very much.

She said, "Maria, how come you never told me this"?

I explained to her that I did not recall it for years and knew that when I brought it out in the open, it would change everyone's life forever.

I did not know how to cope with the emotions that were rising within me.

It was overwhelming!

In those moments, I understood on deeper levels in why the memories of the sexual abuse were not retrieved until later in my life.

It was too much for my mind, heart and body to handle.

The emotional pain that was before me after revealing and confronting my father was going to be heavy and I needed to be ready to handle it going forward on my journey to healing.

After I revealed the painful emotions, I had been holding onto for my entire life, she said to me, "I am going to have my macaroni now." She hung up.

There was no compassion from her for what I had been going through.

She did not call me for 3 days and then showed up at my door with all her negative experiences with my father over the years. She never once acknowledged what I may have been feeling, rather just focused on her own problems she had with him during her marriage.

She told me he had sexual issues, but never explained in detail what they were.

In that moment, I looked at her and did not know who she was.

I wondered where my sweet and loving mother went.

It felt surreal.

I thought to myself, this is NOT my mother.

I did not recognize who she was anymore.

This left me feeling betrayed, unloved, not heard, and

angry!

In that moment I felt she did not believe me.

She was in denial and chose not to hear the truth.

For my mother not to believe me was heart wrenching. In a sense it was more difficult to accept than my father molesting me.

I trusted and loved my mother more than anyone in the world.

She always took loving care of me when I was growing up and I felt love from her.

She remained in the marriage and that was one of the most difficult things for me to accept.

It was a hard pill to swallow.

The betrayal ran deep.

I was devastated!

"No one else can give you the love
you withhold from yourself."

Chapter 7

Silenced

After I confronted my father with the truth of molesting me, there were people in the family who did not believe me.

I understood others cynicism in it all because it came out later in life.

There were so many relatives that did not believe me.

They thought I made it up and falsely recalled it.

I was shocked by their judgements.

Looking back, I realized they were in denial. It was clear.

I felt deeply hurt.

I could not understand, those who knew me for their entire life, questioned my word.

I asked myself, why doesn't anyone believe me?

And for what motive would I have to accuse my father of such a dark act!

I could not comprehend why my relatives did not know my heart.

I felt sad and alone.

Experiencing this by others was by far one of the most difficult feelings to work through.

It is another form of control by others to maintain power over you so that the truth can remain buried.

I found My Voice

My therapist once told me, "It is none of your business what their soul chooses."

That one sentence would help me get through the disappointment and sadness I had felt on a multitude of levels.

It also started to change my victim mentality, "why me"?

I strongly understood that what others chose belongs to them.

It was between them and God.

The hurt they caused had nothing to do with me, it was a reflection of their own unhealed pain.

I cried a river of tears.

During those years, I started to stand strong. I began to believe in myself.

I listened to the inner voice that kept telling me to keep moving forward.

I started to speak the truth aloud. I was no longer concerned with what the opinions of others were of me.

What I came to understand was that no one has any power over you unless you allow it.

It was freeing.

I now had a voice for all those who were willing to listen.

Never be afraid to speak the truth, no matter how others perceive your feelings.

Just be YOU!

The truth releases the sorrow and brings healing to the wounded heart.

Always honor who you are and believe in yourself.

"Boundaries are not walls. They are doors that only let in what aligns with your peace."

Chapter 8
The Power of Words

The Power of Words

When you have suffered verbal abuse, the words being said hurt and affect you psychologically, resulting in emotional abuse.

When someone says something that is ugly or damaging to your psyche, you absorb its energy.

Deep inside you know it is not true and understand it is a projection of the other person's pain being tossed your way, so they can feel empowered.

Nevertheless, it feels awful.

It cuts like a knife in your heart.

You store the degrading words around with you in your mind.

They pop up at the most inconvenient times when you are trying to move on and heal from them.

They reverberate the feelings and thoughts

"I am not worthy of love".

"I am not enough ".

When they do, they are a strong reminder that no one deserves to be devalued or disrespected by anyone, ever!

Words carry energy and whether the verbal abuse is name calling or the degradation of your heart, it can be damaging.

I have experienced this throughout my life.

When it would happen, I was always in disbelief in how it was delivered.

I been called despicable names by multiple people I have known over the course of my life.

Now, when those disparaging words were said to me, it left a feeling of complete and utter devaluation in my being.

I felt small, saddened, and dismissed.

I would fire back in the moment as a knee jerk reaction, but afterwards realizing I lowered myself to that level of energy.

I didn't like how it made me feel.

However, in those unsettling moments, I knew I could not just stand there and not respond to the shocking words of disgust.

I have also experienced verbal abuse from others regarding my appearance and accomplishments throughout the duration of my life which affected me emotionally.

It taught me who they were, and where they lived inside their mind and heart.

Intentional Words

When someone sets out to intentionally hurt you with their words, it is a reminder to never allow this behavior in your life.

It will never bring anything healthy to your inner world, rather it will disrupt your mind, cause confusion, sadness and feelings of unworthiness.

When we speak to another, it needs to come from a place of pure intention.

Speak with integrity.

Voice the energy and the intention of your words

from a place inside you that expresses your truth that flows in the direction of love.

You will be heard.

Chapter 9

Courage

"Courage: the most important of all virtues because without courage, you can't practice any other virtue consistently."

-Maya Angelou-

Courage

Finding courage to move forward, when your support system is weak, is difficult.

This is when you must trust that the pain you are going through will eventually pass.

There were times when I felt I was not going to make it through all the hurt, confusion, and drama I was living.

I was stuck in fear and anger.

I had to find the courage to move on and get on with the rest of my life.

I wondered if I had the strength to continue.

What I found was that I had a reservoir of inner strength that I never knew existed.

The various past relationships kept me drowning in victim mentality, anger, and exhaustion.

Years prior to recalling sexual abuse, I found myself in unhealthy relationships stemming from my unhealed pain as a child.

I was dependent on my husband financially and felt I did not have the capabilities to care for my young children at that time, in providing them with a house.

I was a stay-at-home mother.

I married young and had no skill.

Leaving my marriage while taking the the deep dive into the unknown and trusting that God had my back, was my saving grace.

I graduated from college as an Occupational Therapist and became independent and self-reliant.

I made the choice to take care of myself which brought me freedom to be me and carry on with my life in ways I hadn't experienced yet.

I eventually bought my own home and was able to provide for my children as a single parent.

I was learning to love who I was.

Choices

Making choices to live a healthy life is not an easy road when you have experienced abuse.

Your shattered foundation creates displaced emotions that seeped through the cracks of your mind and heart.

It is like walking on eggshells. Each step is fragile.

Your fears put up a roadblock on your path.

If you step too hard, you fear you will break. If you step too lightly, you fear you will not reach your destination.

Either way, moving forward with tenacity or gen-

"I stopped asking why things happened to me and started asking what I could learn from them."

tly choosing the next step, both will bring you back to YOU.

It does not matter how you GET THERE!

Just move forward every day and begin shedding the pain you have experienced.

Learn to forgive yourself for the choices you have made based on your abusive past.

It is okay to fail and make mistakes.

Most importantly, releasing those who made you lose sight of yourself and brought confusion to your mind and heart.

Place the focus on yourself, choosing what is always best for you.

Change your victim mentality mindset and replace it with love for yourself.

Choose YOU!

Chapter 10

Illusions

We unconsciously create illusions to stifle our progress based on our fears.

When we feed into the illusion, our life comes to a dead halt.

We live life going through the motions and not feeling our soul's essence.

We become robots in our daily routine and stop living the life that we came here to experience.

I lived illusions in my relationships.

I unconsciously created these illusions to starve my deepest desires, so I did not have to look at myself.

I kept wanting things to be different, waiting for those I cared deeply about to change, to be heard and to get my needs fulfilled.

What I found was you cannot change anyone.

You can only change yourself.

When you change yourself inside, you change your energy.

When you do, you start attracting what you need because you awakened to your truth energetically and cleared the path to your deepest desires.

The Universe begins to respond to the shift you

have consciously chosen for yourself.

Nothing external can create what you desire and give you what you need.

It all begins within YOU!

Decisions

When you make the conscious choice to heal yourself, you are letting God and the universe know you are ready to move forward to the next step in your soul's growth.

You wake up to the unconscious life you have been living.

Your higher self will bring you to the next phase of your life when you find the strength to move forward and decide that the current life of misery no longer serves your heart and soul.

One decision can change the course of your life in ways you never, ever could imagine!

Chapter 11

Letting Go

Letting go was one of my biggest lessons in life.

God kept bringing me to situations where I had to decide to let go of what I was holding onto so tightly!

It goes back to trying to be in control of everything.

When you ignore the inner work that needs to be done, you remain in this mindset.

Control is the resistance to what needs healing.

It can destroy relationships, your soul's progression and bring you nothing but heartache.

When you try to control the outcome of any situation, you will suffer.

It is the fear of the unknown that you are trying to control.

You must release the resistance to the deep pain and surrender.

The only one in control is your higher self through God.

Your ego tries to control the outcome, but it is your higher self that is in charge.

"Healing is not a straight line. It's a dance of falling and rising, breaking and rebuilding."

Surrendering your fears to the universe is the greatest choice you will ever make.

It takes unwavering trust to give it up to a higher power greater than your personality and ego.

The only thing you can control is yourself.

Your choices, decisions and reactions are within your reach. Dig deep.

Choose with your higher self and look through the lens of discernment.

Release it over and allow source energy to guide you through to the path of love.

Trust in YOU!

Trust

When you begin to trust in the decisions to create your own healthy path, you will start having trust in others, but most importantly, you will begin to trust in yourself.

Trust has been a life- long lesson of mine.

Not only did I not trust myself, but I also did not trust the process of life's unfolding.

Fear was my companion.

I did not feel safe, protected, loved or supported in the direction of my life.

My foundation had so many cracks in it, I had no idea who I was and how to manage myself.

I had been lied to on multiple occasions in relationships of all kinds that I placed my love, trust and energy into.

When a person you love and care about looks you straight in the eyes and lies to you, it is hard to get past it.

The trust you held within falls by the wayside and uncertainty arises inside of you.

Betrayal by my parents and mistrust in a variety of personal relationships over the years resulted in my inability to trust

I had such unhealed pain from the trust being broken at 5 years of age by my father molesting me that often times in personal relationships, I felt that I was being cheated on by those I cared for.

I didn't feel loved. I needed to love myself.

What I realized was that I was cheating and betraying myself by allowing the mistreatment by others.

I learned along the way that I needed to be courageous and trust in the process of life.

I needed to trust myself and the guidance I was receiving.

Always heed the call to your higher self that is attempting to break through the barriers of fear and bring you to healing.

When something does not feel right, listen to that guidance! Do not ignore what you are receiving.

This is your soul speaking to you.

When I ignored what I was receiving over the years, I only hurt myself. The same lessons continued to repeat themselves.

Your higher self will only give you what you need.

Trust it with all your being! It will Never fail you.

Chapter 12

Hear My Word

"And whenever you stand praying, if you have anything against anyone, forgive him."
-Jesus-

Hear My Word
On November 27th, 2011, I had a dream of Jesus.
I was standing there all alone in the dream.
Suddenly, Jesus spoke to me in my right ear.
He said, "Maria, this is Jesus. Hear my word."
HIS voice was unforgettable!

When I awakened, I felt humbled that Jesus visited me in my dream with his message!
I knew in my heart, when I woke up that the message Jesus was conveying to me was about forgiveness so I can heal and move forward from the pain.

I had not forgiven my father nor my mother for the pain they both caused me throughout my journey.
I was still holding onto the anger and did not know how to release it.

Honestly, I never read the Bible before, nor do I consider myself religious. I was not sure if Jesus ever said "Hear My Word" in its writings.

I decided to look up his words online that morning and searched on google, "Hear My Word." This is what I found.

"Why do you not understand what I say? It is because you cannot bear to hear my word."

I was taken back by the dream visit from Jesus.

Even though I did not want to hear what Jesus was asking me to do, I was eternally grateful for his incredible presence and message.

Forgiveness

I was having such a challenging time forgiving my father and mother.

I would constantly wonder how could I forgive such betrayal?

The emotional pain ran deep to the core of my being.

If you cannot trust your parents, then whom can you trust?

When your parents betray your very soul, it is not easy to heal.

This is when you place your trust in God.

You must find the lesson in the betrayal and embrace it.

I had to find a way to forgive my parents for their acts of betrayal I felt deep within me.

Forgiving them was not ever about giving them a pass or an excuse for the betrayal, rather it was for me.

It was a channel for me to release and allow the pain to just be and for me not to carry the anger anymore.

When I began to forgive, I was able to start moving away from the consuming thoughts of their actions towards me, I began to contemplate more on my healing.

I started to take my focus off the ruminating thoughts and feelings I had about them and turn them inwards, placing my center of attention on what I needed.

My mother's betrayal consumed my heart because I needed her to be there for me.

When she wasn't and decided to stay with my father after the confrontation, it created a deeper wound than what I already was carrying.

What I came to understand was that my mother did not have the tools to heal from the abuse she suffered from my father.

My father emotionally abused her. He cheated on her and treated her badly over the years.

He would give her the silent treatment. Watching her experience the silent treatment over the years was gut wrenching.

I finally understood her roadblocks, her mindset, and her inability to move on from him. She was an abused spouse.

"There is strength in softness, power in vulnerability, and courage in letting yourself be seen."

After she had died, that is when I was able to fully release the pain I had carried.

When I got home from her funeral, I went and sat on the top of a mountain near where I lived.

The grief I felt was indescribable!

I never cried or felt this type of deep sadness before.

I wept for hours.

During these moments I thanked my mother for giving me life and taking care of me until the day I left the house and went off on my own.

I let her know through my heart that I loved her and always would.

I told her I forgive her for how she made me feel.

I released a lot of hurt that day on the mountain.

My father's horrific choice to molest me when I was five years old brought me to my knees.

His horrendous actions would remain with me throughout my life creating one downfall after another.

Until I decided to heal and do the work, life continued to be a struggle in relationships and in loving myself.

It guided me back to what I needed to do. I needed to acknowledge and allow to feel the Overwhelming pain.

It was a tough road to journey along.

But I made it!

I was able to let go of the intense hurt and forgive them both.

Forgiving them meant I could move forward. I was able to detach and feel indifferent towards them.

This process took many years to achieve.

I distanced myself from my mother over those years until she died. I loved her but could not engage in the living arrangement she was in with my father.

It was a constant reminder of the betrayal.

I had no relationship with my father since the day of the confrontation.

I realized that holding onto the anger would only hurt me if I stayed stuck in that energy.

I no longer gave them power over me by the choices their souls made.

I was beginning to get my power back.

I was starting to heal in small ways.

Chapter 13

Healing Dream

Healing Dream

I knew I was on the road to healing when I had this dream in my late forties. I had shared the dream with my therapist in a session with her.

In the dream, I was my five-year-old self, walking along a sidewalk. Approaching me was a little girl who looked exactly like me when I was five.

She had deep, dark brown hair, straight bangs and was petit.

I went up to her and asked her what her name was. I told her she looked just like me.

She said, "My name is Maria, and I told her so is mine!" We hugged each other and we both said at the same time, "I love you "and then walked away holding hands together as we skipped down the sidewalk.

My therapist told me that the dream represented me loving myself. She said I did not need to return for therapy anymore.

She recognized I was on the road to self-love and moving away from anger and victim mentality.

"Gentleness is not weakness; it's the quiet strength that opens hearts, heals wounds, and lights the path to true connection."

My soul met up with my higher self in a dream state to remind me of who I am and that I am lovable.

My heart was beginning to open.

Healing

Healing begins with releasing the past and embracing self-love. The road to self-love is a process learned through self-reflection, setting strong boundaries and letting go of the pain. Healing means surrendering to what happened and knowing that it was not your fault, you were abused.

When your life has been saturated by drama, healing cannot take place. Ironically, it's the drama that will eventually lead you to healing.

This happens because you will reach the point where living a life of drama holds no love, peace or authenticity.

It is exhausting and full of emptiness.

It wears on you physically, emotionally, and mentally.

When I was in the height of the drama I created through my choices, my body started to break down.

I got vertigo.

Interestingly, the symptom of vertigo is a sensation of the room spinning which was a metaphor that my life was spinning out of control.

I was losing my balance.

When you hold in unreleased hurt, sadness and pain, your body stores these unhealed emotions, keeping the energy from flowing together, creating illness in the cells of the body.

The body is a living organism of energy and needs

to be in a state of homeostasis to remain in balance.

The body FEELS the emotions that you are feeling. An example is when you hear or see something sad, you feel it in your heart area of the body. Your body is having a visceral reaction to the emotion that you are feeling.

It is important to care for the mind, body, and spirit as a whole being.

They are not separate from each other.

They are in synchrony with one another. When one part is tipping the scale of emotions too far to the left, the other parts are trying to balance the scale to the right creating equilibrium of body, mind, and spirit.

When you are out of alignment emotionally, it will show up physically in the body.

Realizing this, I needed to directly peer into the souls of my eyes to begin the healing journey to myself.

The veil of denial was lifting.

Chapter 14
Releasing The Pain

"Just let go. Let go of how you thought your life was supposed to be and embrace the life that is trying to work its way into your consciousness."

-Caroline Myss-

Releasing the Pain

Letting go of the pain is one of the hardest things to do when you are hurting.

I spent years holding on to all the betrayal and deep-rooted sadness for what happened.

I wanted to know why and how this could have occurred. I needed answers.

What I did not understand at the time was that my continual residence in the pain was not only hurting others, but most importantly it was preventing me from living a life of love, truth, joy and peace.

I finally had to let it all go and asked God and the Universe to direct me out of this nightmare of emptiness that lived inside of me.

I started to understand on a deeper level that I had to move on and focus on what makes me happy.

To do this I had to take a deep dive into my soul and cleanse what had been holding me back for years from moving on.

This was not easy to do. It involved going within and feeling all those activating triggers that came on throughout the healing process.

It felt like I was falling through a black hole with no end in sight. I felt the colossal void of betrayal and the emptiness I had been carrying.

It was a hollowing feeling. When the activation of the betrayal occurred, I had to literally vomit.

I realized every time I was triggered by the past, I had to sit with those feelings and cry a waterfall of tears to release them.

Sitting with the feelings of being devalued and discarded by your parents and my failed relationships was one of darkness.

The feeling left me with an emptiness that is indescribable. It was void of light or love.

 It was the utter absence of God and the true disconnection to my higher self.

This kind of betrayal felt like a tight spun web of emotions becoming entangled and enmeshed in the pain.

To untangle them was difficult but necessary to heal.

I had to feel it all and let it go.

Balance
Finding my center in the chaos was a true learn-

ing experience. It was easy to be thrown off balance in the height of the drama. This balancing act to get centered and to stay non-reactive became a daily skill of my mind and heart.

- When I was triggered, I would begin to observe my reactions to things and try not to react to them. I would reflect on those triggered feelings and exam them closely into the source of pain.

What I would find in the unraveling of the pain was that more healing needed to take place. The layers were buried down far into my being.

These layers of healing are on a continuum. Shedding them with care, support and self-love is crucial in the healing process.

When the triggers subside and lessen in frequency, so does the pain.

I would remind myself that I am worthy of love and the receiving of it. I had to find a way to give it to myself and to turn my focus on what made me feel good. It was a daily practice.

Eventually I found my center and was able to maintain it or at the very least get back to it quicker when it revealed itself again.

I was healing. I felt a shift within me. I no longer was attached to the past nor the players in it.

Chapter 15

The Healing Power of Crying

The Healing Power of Crying

When we are hurting, we feel inundated with pain inside ourselves.

It feels like filling up a water balloon to its maximal content and tying the knot at the end of the balloon.

The balloon cannot hold any more water, or it will break open.

Just as you experience the painful emotions that are building inside you from abuse.

They are being held there, needing an outlet.

Crying is God's natural, innate way of self-healing. It releases the sadness and gives the energy inside the body a path to flow more freely breaking down the dam of emotions that have been built through great discomfort and disbelief.

Feel your tears drip down your cheeks cleansing your pain and feeling the power within your soul.

Releasing Through Joy

Not only is crying God's natural source of self-healing but so is laughing.

Laughter is the greatest medicine for pain.

"The past shaped me, but it does not define me. I am free to choose my own path."

When we laugh, it goes through the heart and opens its blocked energy and settles down into the stomach area.

Have you ever laughed so hard that your stomach muscles hurt?

I have and it is an extraordinary experience of pure joy!

God built in these forms of release into our bodies to allow the energy within to continue to flow smoothly, so the resistance is lifted inside ourselves.

Always feel your pain, sit with it and release it through tears and laughter.

You will feel like a balloon being launched into the sky and be freed of the stored painful emotions you have tightly held onto.

Freedom of your true self will be felt! Stay present and enjoy who you truly are!

Chapter 16

Being Ready

Being Ready

When others try to help you in your confusion and pain and you are unable to receive their input, it lets you know that you are not ready to go to the next level of healing.

When you decide that you do not want to feel a certain way anymore, then, and only then can you shift your energy to the next phase in the process.

You must be ready to hear the guidance your higher self is trying to express, otherwise you will remain stuck.

Nothing anyone can tell you will penetrate through your consciousness.

You must do it yourself!

You need to make the choice to feel good and stay present to enjoy who you truly are.

I eventually reached this point, and my life started to flow in the direction of love, healing, and joy.

"For the first time, I am not running from my past—I am walking forward with my future."

Finding Your Way Through

After living a life of hurt, confusion, and betrayal, I finally reached a place where there was no room for abuse of any kind.

There was only room for self-love, respect, kindness and truth.

I finally saw everything.

It was as though the Light was turned on and the darkness dissipated into the ethers of nothingness.

The clarity of discernment became the front line of my protection in feeling safe in my own skin.

I no longer would allow myself to be abused, manipulated or devalued by anyone.

Learning how to establish strong boundaries was a lifesaver for my being.

I finally found the freedom and peace I had been desiring for my entire life.

Chapter 17

The Purity of Love

When you have suffered abuse, your awareness of healthy relationships becomes dimmed, and you lose sight of what is tolerable and what is not.

You tolerate disrespect, verbal, emotional and physical abuse because your mind becomes shrouded in confusion.

My role model of love growing up was out of alignment with my true self. It was a misconception of what love truly was.

When abuse of all kinds is experienced, the tolerance of disrespect feels "normal", In a twisted way, there is a familiar unconscious comfort in it all.

You set out into the world seeking love in relationships, only to find out that the love you seek needs to come from within you.

Until you love yourself, no relationship of any kind could truly be healthy.

You must love yourself first and when you do, your heart will open to the love that is the truth.

Relationships and experiences of all kinds will begin unfolding in your life showing you what true love represents.

True unconditional love is about having mutual understanding for one another, sharing open communication, honesty, truth, loyalty, feeling safe, respect, encouragement, trust, patience, and kindness. You value each other for who you are.

It demonstrates an exchange of shared, reciprocated, and balanced energy.

Unconditional love is the inward reflection of God, revealing itself outwardly through your words, intentions, actions, and behaviors towards one another.

This allows for an open channel to just be ourselves with each other.

Trust in the Universe

"All I have seen teaches me to trust the creator for all I have not seen."

-Ralph Waldo Emerson-

One of my biggest lessons was to learn to trust.

I needed to learn to trust in myself, but most importantly to trust in God's messages I had been receiving.

I found I had a difficult time trusting in a variety of relationships that presented themselves over the years.

I would carry that fear unconsciously into many relationships and ultimately attract that mistrust into my life.

I ignored all the red flags that the universe was sending me to not tolerate abuse.

The messages that were being given were loud and

"What once felt like endings were actually beginnings in disguise."

clear. They were about loving myself.

We attract what we believe to be true.
What we believe, we become.
Our mind is a powerful tool.
The inner dialogue we have with ourselves that our mind and emotions reveal, allows the universe to respond with the energy we give it.
It sends back what we have asked for.
If you think and feel negative, that is what will be returned to your life.
The opposite is true. If you are thinking and feeling positive, that is what will manifest.

It is called the law of attraction.
Like attracts like.
It is universal law.
My continual residence in the pain and my inability to get out of my own way, kept me in the same patterns of unhealthy relationships.
Subconsciously, I did not believe or trust I was worthy of love.
In return, that is what I attracted back to me.
Until I understood that I was the creator of my own reality by the thoughts, feelings, and beliefs that I carried within me from my childhood, my relationships remained the same, empty and unfulfilled.
I subconsciously created what I believed to be true.
I did not trust in my higher self.
I betrayed myself in the process.

Chapter 18
The Internal Work

Going through the trauma of sexual abuse as a child created a lifelong problem of confusion.

One day you feel you learned the lessons of the past, then out of nowhere, the lessons resurface.

You feel you are healthy and learned the lessons of the past only to find out it came back to test you.

You wonder how this could be happening again.

The universe will continue to send the same experiences until they are learned.

The inner work involves delving deep into the pain.

You must uncover the root of the problem that continues bringing up the same patterns of abuse that kept you stuck for years.

To dive deep into the pain requires you to be fully honest with yourself and take off the blinders that have been covering up the pain.

You must allow yourself to feel all the emotions and release them.

Check in with your feelings and ask yourself why these emotions are surfacing again.

Triggers are messages of unhealed pain that lives

"Joy is not the absence of pain;
it is the presence of love and the
courage to begin again."

inside of you.

You may be triggered by others hurtful actions, behaviors, and words.

If someone says something or does something to hurt you,

It is letting you know that healing needs to take place.

If you continue ignoring the triggers, the same patterns will reoccur.

Learned Lessons

I had so many insecurities growing up from sexual abuse that I carried them into my life as an adult.

I had no confidence. As a child and young adult, I was very shy and was afraid to express myself.

As I began to become aware of my traumas and what needed to heal, I learned how to give love to my core self.

I learned that all my relationships taught me who I am and what I desired in them.

I learned to have a voice.

I learned self-reliance.

I learned what triggered me and how to heal those triggers.

I learned not to respond or react to abuse of any kind.

I learned to drop the illusions that kept me blinded and to see the truth.

I learned how to create strong boundaries.

I learned to trust what I was perceiving with great clarity and to listen to that discernment.

I learned to say NO.

I learned to have faith in the guidance I was receiving and to act on it.

I learned that give and take was an equal exchange of energy and that is what I desired in all relationships.

I learned to let others go with love and let them be who they are.

I learned not to take anything personal.

I learned balance in all areas of my life.

I learned I was lovable.

I learned to stand in my truth.

I learned that words from others must match behaviors otherwise it has no authentic meaning.

I learned that what I believe at my core, I will attract into my life.

I learned endurance and resilience.

I learned that the negativity you hold in your mind continues to reveal itself until it is transformed into love and wisdom.

I learned self compassion.

I learned that what you allow will continue in the forms of abuse until the allowance transcends into awareness and self love.

I learned to love who I am with all my human imperfections.

I learned that I was the only one who can make the choice to heal myself.

I learned on the deepest level in my soul that I am a part of God and that I am whole just as I am.

I learned self-love.

Chapter 19

"Gratitude is not only the greatest of virtues, but the parent of all others."
-Marcus Tullius Cicero-

Gratitude

Gratitude is a magnet to your higher self and brings to you all that your soul is seeking.

Being grateful for all your experiences in life is one of the best prayers you can send out to the Universe.

During my struggles to heal, the one thing that brought me directly to God and to my true essence was the feeling of gratitude for the pain.

I understood that what happened to me as a child brought me to myself, my true self.

I had to go through painful lessons to reach my core. This was my path.

I was grateful for finding a way out of the pain which gave me great insight into learning how to love myself and not tolerate any form of abuse of any kind.

I am grateful for its entirety.

When you feel gratitude for everything in life and for your existence here on earth, it shifts your energy directly to God. It will immediately change your limiting perspectives into positive ones that otherwise would have kept you paralyzed in negativity.

Gratitude frees the mind and sets the soul soaring.

Unconditional Love

Love is an energy that flows through you and from you.

When you are open to receiving and giving it to yourself and others, it becomes a way of living.

Love is the superpower we all have innately.

Tap into its energy.

Give it to yourself and all those you adore and care about.

Allow yourself to receive it in times of heartache and confusion.

When you open that door to universal love, your life will flow in the direction of it.

Stay in the energy current of love.

It will be your guide to your Higher Self!

Chapter 20

The Meaning of Self-Love

It means doing whatever brings you joy.

It means being selfish enough to choose YOU.

It means keeping your word to yourself and to others.

It means saying NO.

It means not betraying yourself.

It means creating strong boundaries.

It means detaching from the pain and surrendering to your higher self.

It means self-respect and forgiveness.

It means not tolerating anything that does not feel good to you.

It means being present and enjoying your time alone.

It means making healthy choices that serve your needs.

It means listening and connecting to your higher self.

It means being grateful for all your difficult lessons in life.

"*The moment I stopped seeking validation from others was the moment I became truly free.*"

It means remaining in your own energy and feeling safe there.

It means staying in your true power.

It means trusting in the divine unfolding.

It means being true to yourself.

It means not allowing others to disturb your peace.

It means knowing the God in YOU!

It means that YOU are the reflection of LOVE itself.

It means choosing YOU!

Choosing Joy

"Where your attention goes, your energy flows"
-James Redfield-

Creating joy in your life is one of the most loving things you can do for yourself.

Feeling joyful is why we are here on earth. We came here to experience joy in all aspects of life.

When we choose to feel happy, we will attract that energy to ourselves.

We energetically attract what we believe to be true within us.

Another words, if you are sad, angry or resentful and you remain with those feelings long term, then you become stuck in that energy.

Even when you are going through challenging times, try your best to feel good.

You will find a shift in energy when you remain focused on that good feeling.

As you practice ITS good feeling, you will receive more of it, day by day.

Our mind is powerful. What we feed it, it digests and travels through our energy holding us in that space.

Live in joy!

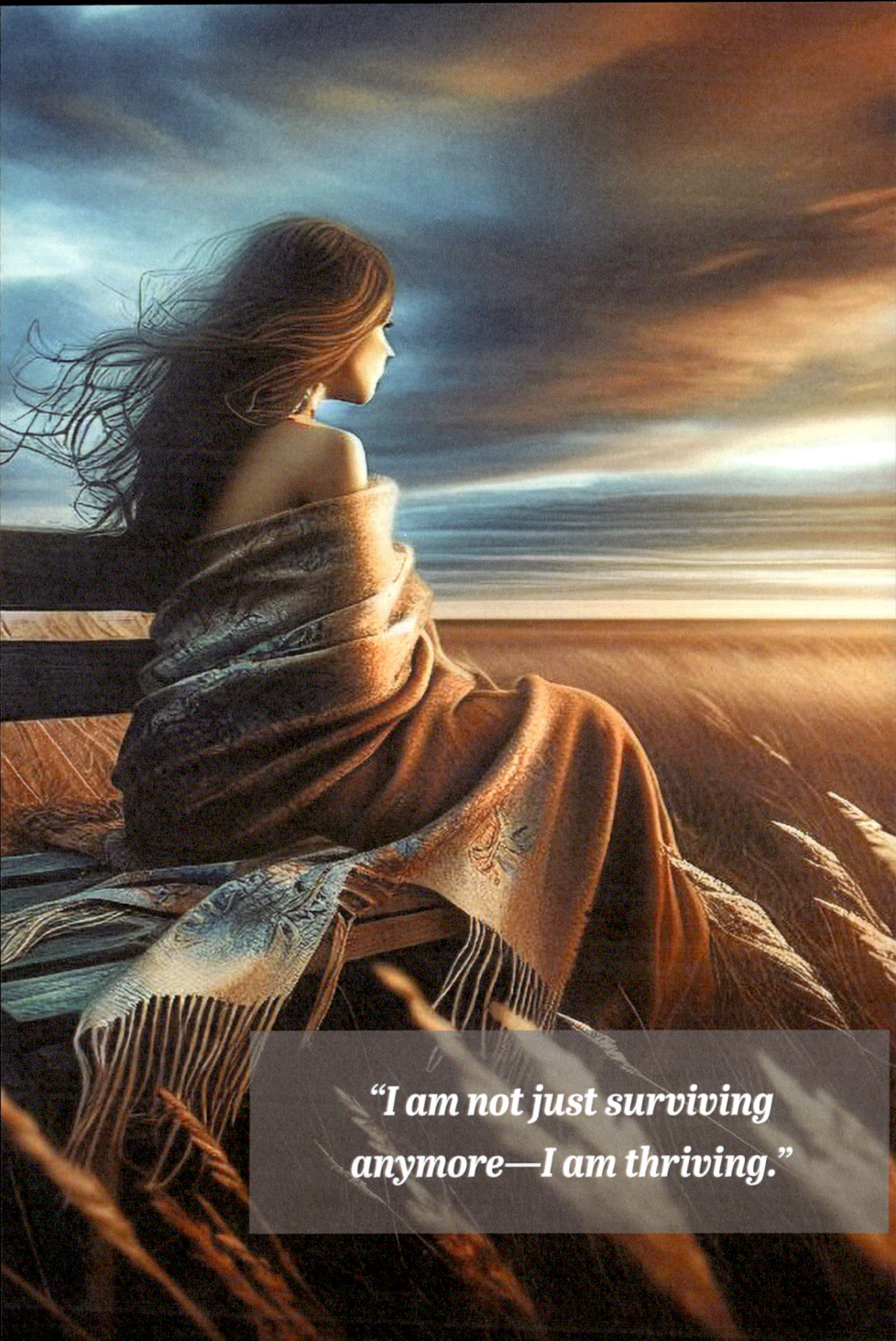

"I am not just surviving anymore—I am thriving."

Chapter 21

Peace

To live a peaceful existence is to be present and live peacefully.

You cannot attract peace unless you demonstrate it to yourself.

Peace comes with letting go of the control.

When you allow to trust in the divine plan that is set out before you, peace arrives.

Always love yourself and choose love, it will never misguide you.

Remove all things from your life that do not serve your soul.

Be honest with yourself and be vulnerable to heeding the call to what feels uncomfortable so healing can take place.

Meditate and rest your mind, body and heart.

Journal your feelings.

Release all those with love who have caused you pain and understand that each of them was operating on the level of consciousness that they were in at the time.

Remain in your center and stay balanced.

Resonate in the stillness in the center of your heart and remain there.

Freedom
Live in the moment.
Be present in all experiences in your life.
Dance and sing your heart out.
Laugh, cry, love.
Heal yourself.
Share your heart and be vulnerable.
Be joyful.
Lift yourself up and go on an adventure.
Be playful, while feeling the essence of it.
Take a walk in nature and see
GOD in everything and in YOU.
Transcend your pain into a profound sense of self love.
Do things you love that fill your heart up.
Live without regret.

Surrender control.

Feel the newly founded clarity and carry it with you in all experiences in life.

Express your deepest thoughts and feelings from your soul with others.

Create something that reflects your energy and share it with all those you love.

Be still and feel the universe and God within you.

Detach yourself from anything that causes confusion, conflict or negativity and bring yourself to the present moment feeling the ease within you.

Flow with the energy of synchronicity and watch miracles unfold right before your very eyes as the universe delivers them to you.

Know that all of life is a learning experience to elevate your soul and that everything that happens is for the sole purpose to experience YOU in all your beauty and creation.

"Happiness was never something I had to chase. It was something I had to allow."

Chapter 22

Just Be You

All you ever need to do in life is to just be yourself.

Always know from the depths of your soul that you are enough just as you are.

You do not have to prove yourself to anyone nor seek validation from others to know your worth.

Never allow anyone to disrespect or manipulate your heart.

Always stand in your truth and speak it.

Living your authentic self is the most loving and freeing choice you can make.

Do not allow anyone to burnout your light.

Do not ever lose sight of who you truly are!

Know Thyself

"Knowing yourself is the beginning of all wisdom."
-Aristotle-

Knowing who YOU are and expressing that out in the world is the greatest gift you can give to yourself and others.

YOU are an eternal being experiencing yourself on earth to learn all you can to elevate your soul through the different experiences you encounter.

It is not enough to have a mental construct of what needs to take place, rather you must walk through the pain and feel it.

You must feel it to heal it!

Cry and release the abuse that you have held on tightly, preventing you from being your true self.

The Universe will test you to be sure you got it.

The lessons will resurface, and red flags will start waving quickly in front of you.

Pay attention to them. Listen to your inner voice. Follow your higher self.

You will know when you have reached the other side of the pain when you become aware of YOU, your traumas of abuse, the patterns that kept you locked in place and the energy that held you there.

When the awareness settles in and healing has taken place through the internal work of your being, an energy shift happens within you.

A peaceful feeling becomes anchored in your soul.

It is yours to keep and is not open for disturbance.

It resonates within even during times of emotional upsets.

It is your personal compass to the center of your heart!

Chapter 23

Soul Questions

When we reflect, self-examination appears.

As you go through the healing process be fully honest with yourself when answering these questions.

Why won't I let go?
What am I afraid of?
What is it I don't trust?
What do I need?

What don't I want to see?
Do I care what others think of me and if so, why do I care?

What are my beliefs?
Why do I believe the negative voice in my head?
Where did these negative thoughts originate from?
Who am I really?
What is it that I am seeking?
What is Love and what does it feel like to me when it takes form?
How do I want to feel when I am loved by another?
What do I try to control and why?
Is what I want, what I need?
What am I trying to prove to myself?

"You are not the pain you endured. You are the strength that carried you through it, the light that refused to be dimmed. The future is yours—walk into it with love and certainty."

Write down the answers to these questions.

When we take time within the silence of our soul, the answers will come to us.

Listen closely!

Soul Healing

"By changing your perception, you can change your reality".

-Dr. Bruce Lipton-

When you believe in yourself, you are set free.

Never buy into negative self-talk. It is all a lie.

• In my early years as a child, teenager, and adult, I lived with this internal lie. I did not believe in myself.

The negative self-talk stemmed from the sexual abuse and the environments I chose to be surrounded by which were carried over throughout the years of my life.

I finally realized who I was and began believing in my value. I realized it was me who was creating the self-dialogue which allowed the continuing of negativity in my mind.

The only person who could break these chains of self-imprisonment is YOU!

Value your life, yourself and everything sent your way.

They are all messages from your higher self to assist you in seeing who you truly are.

Unlock your limiting beliefs that have created a

recording in your subconscious that played a repeated tape saying you were not worthy of love.

Make a new recording every day that YOU are worthy of love and a life filled with joy and abundance!

Repeat, Play, Repeat.

We are energetic beings.

We can feel energies that come into our awareness through the vibrations of frequencies that flow through us.

We can become aware at any given moment where we are on the emotional scale.

When you take a moment to stop and reflect in why you are feeling a certain way, awareness comes to our attention.

These frequencies are connected with the level of emotions we experience every day.

When you go through the scale, feel the energy of each emotion.

Emotions are energy in motion.

You will find that each level of emotion, whether it is riding the lower frequencies or higher ones, that your emotions direct you in how you feel and set in motion behaviors that match that emotion.

I feel this scale will be a helpful tool in determining where your emotions reside and how to elevate your frequency to assist with healing.

This scale was created by Esther/Abraham-Hicks.

It is called The Emotional Guidance Scale.

The highest frequency of emotions starts at the top of the scale and works its way down towards the lower frequencies which are at the low end of the scale.

In retrospect when I reflect on the years, when I was feeling victimized, betrayed, confused and angry, I can now understand where I was operating from and how living in these lower frequencies kept me stuck in the energy of stagnation.

When you plug into higher levels of frequencies and remain there to the best of your ability, your subconscious will play it back to you.

Pay attention each day to where you are at any given moment on the scale of emotions and make adjustments according to your specific needs at that time Go through each emotion and note how it makes you feel inside. Stay on the course to higher consciousness and frequencies to who you truly are. Your life will unfold moment by moment with love, truth and joy when you do the inner work. Where are you on the emotional scale?

Chapter 24

A Journey To Self Discovery

"It takes courage to endure the sharp pains of self-discovery rather than to choose to take the dull pain of unconsciousness that would last the rest of our lives".

Marianne Williamson-

A Journey to Self-Discovery

The journey to healing is not an easy one.

It is a process of awareness, learning, unlearning, allowing, living, growing and releasing.

The most expansive part of the journey for YOU is the richness of the experiences themselves.

Without the experience, there would be nothing to learn.

To embrace this journey, you must uncover your limiting beliefs and patterns you have held onto and begin to shed away each layer of illusion, betrayal, self-hatred, sadness, disbelief, anger, and confusion.

When it becomes overwhelming, do not give up. Perseverance will push you forward in the direction of healing.

Your resilience will surprise you.

Find the support through the love of your friends, family, a spiritual counselor and a trained therapist.

You also may want to explore alternative therapies that resonate with your soul to complement your healing process.

I found hypnotherapy to be a remarkable alternative therapy in the final release of hidden unconscious blocks that held me back from being who I truly am.

It was a mind blowing experience and synchronistically enchanting!

Awakening the Soul

When you become aware of the unhappiness you been experiencing, your soul will call upon you to take a different path.

It won't be easy at first to take the call to transformation. The unknown will feel uncomfortable and uneasy.

You will keep feeling a shift of energy within yourself that keeps whispering to your soul to move on from the pain of the past.

Pay close attention to this. It is your soul speaking through you.

Answer the call. Don't place it on hold. Do not hang up.

Receive the voice message of self-love that is being sent from your higher self.

YOU will feel a weightlessness that lifts you up inside.

You no longer will carry the burdens that have gripped you forever.

When you look back, you will see all the snapshots of your life.

View them as a photo album of all your souls' experiences. During introspection, look at the flash prints in your minds eye as they appear before you, seeing your experiences at the different stages in life.

Take note to what you are viewing and feeling.

Each image will tell a story of where you were on your soul's journey back to LOVE.

After experiencing this, you will feel the essence of each moment reminding you what your soul has experienced.

You may not recognize yourself anymore.

Your heart will reveal the healing insight and wisdom that you have acquired along the way through the journey of your soul.

Reintroduce yourself to YOU.

"Hi, it is very nice to meet you and to get to know you".

"I love you".

You will feel your heart's energy opening.

There is a light at the end of the dark tunnel.

That light is YOU!

Be courageous and soar through it with self- love,

forgiveness, truth, trust, gratitude, inner strength and wisdom.

You will find YOU there.
Where YOU always have been.
Right HERE, Right NOW!

Conclusion

Sharing my personal journey of abuse came through from the most profound expressions of my soul.

I had to learn who I was through an array of experiences with abuse.

I healed to the best of my being.

My heartfelt intention in sharing my story was for the sole purpose of knowing that healing and transformation can take place within you.

You are not alone in your painful feelings with your experiences of abuse.

This is NOT who YOU are!

My deep intentions were for these pages to resonate with your soul and that YOU saw a part of yourself within my story.

Know deep within yourself that we can all transform our pain into great love for ourselves.

My greatest desire is that you found inspiration, insight and healing as you read the book.

Through this, know with every part of your being, that remaining in the pain with the past will only keep you held there in that energy, preventing forward motion to the life you came here to live.

Always remember, you are not defined by your abusive past.

It is not your true- identity, rather it changes who you are and clouds your inner beauty.

As you unpack the deep hurtful emotions associated with the abuse and release them, you will awaken to parts of yourself that you never knew existed.

YOU are a unique soul experiencing your true self, which is love at its very core.

Go within NOW and SEE who YOU truly are.

Move on in YOUR truth on your journey back to YOU!

Dedication

I would like to dedicate this book in loving memory, to my dearest, most loving friend, Jeani.
I would not have made it this far without her unconditional love and guidance.
Thank you, Jeani, from the depths of my soul for all YOU have given to me in this lifetime!
Thank you for walking next to me on my path.
I am infinitely grateful for the love and friendship you brought to my heart.
Your love and guidance will forever echo in my soul!
I love YOU with all my being!

"You were my strength when I was weak, you were my voice when I couldn't speak, you were my eyes when I couldn't see, I Am everything I am because you loved me". -Celine Dion

I would also like to thank James Van Praagh, from my heart, for the knowledge I gained from his online class to author this book.
Thank you so much! I am deeply thankful for the inspiration you brought to me.

About The Author

Maria Certo was born and raised in Western New York and now resides in Ventura, where she enjoys the peaceful energy of the coast. A devoted mother of two, she has spent her life navigating personal growth, resilience, and healing. Now retired, Maria dedicates her time to self-discovery, spiritual exploration, and inspiring others to find their own strength and truth. The Transported Soul is a deeply personal journey she felt called to share, offering inspiration and empowerment to those seeking their own path to healing.

Resources

Here are signs of sexual abuse in a child.
Behavioral Signs

- "Acting younger or going back to doing younger tasks and activities.

- "Sudden changes in behavior."
- "Fear of being alone with a certain person."
- "Sudden unexplained fears of certain places or kinds of people."
- "Fear of being touched."
- "Changes in quality of schoolwork or grades."
- "Substance abuse."
- "Delinquency"
- "Self-Mutilation or careless behaviors resulting in self-harm."
- "Excessive play with their own private body parts".
- "Persistent sex play with friends, toys or pets".
- "Frequent drawings that have sexual content."
- "Unusual, persistent, or developmentally inappropriate questioning about human sexuality."

Physical Signs

- "Eating more or less than usual."
- "Having trouble sleeping".
- "Soiling or wetting clothes or bedwetting."
- "Physical pain or itching in the genital areas".
- "Underwear stained with blood or discharge."
- "Rectal bleeding."
- "Problems walking or sitting."

Emotional Signs
"Severe anxiety such as nightmares or clinging."
"Depression such as withdrawal, low self-esteem, thinking about or attempting suicide or frequent crying."
- "Extreme anger (for example, tantrums, aggression or increased irritability)"

This information was founded by Committee for Children in 2024

The National Sexual Assault Hotline
Available 24 hours
1-800-656-4673

About The Illustrator
Suzanne Pell

Suzanne Pell is an illustrator, designer, and publishing consultant who helps authors bring their stories to life from concept to completion. She doesn't just make a book look beautiful—she helps you make it become one. From illustration and layout to formatting, ISBN registration, and publishing setup, Suzanne guides each project through every stage with artistry and care. Known for her warmth, attention to detail, and deep understanding of storytelling, she creates books that feel as meaningful as they are visually striking. You can contact her at sue@booksbysue.com

.

About This Work

Written By Maria Certo
Illustrated & Designed by Suzanne Pell
All Rights Reserved
ISBN # 978-1-969146-11-4
mariatruth333@yahoo.com